EARTHFEST—A CELEBRATION

By

Paul A. Hanson

ISBN : 9780988375932

Copyright 2014 by Paul A. Hanson

Published by the Sheboygan County Historical Research Center, 518 Water Street Sheboygan Falls, WI 53085

INTRODUCTION

President Jimmy Carter during his administration (1977-1981) installed solar panels on the White House roof; when Ronald Reagan became President in 1981, he removed the solar panels. He, also, made a statement that trees cause pollution. What?

When I was an undergraduate at UW-Green Bay, I had a friend who always carried an oversized bag on her shoulder; she used this bag when she went grocery shopping. When the bagger would ask her if she wanted "Paper or plastic," she replied, "Neither," because she brought her own bag. People thought she was strange. Why didn't she use the store's bags? Why did she bring her own? And now, today, a bagger will ask you, "Paper or plastic. Oh, I see, you brought your own." And now, there's nothing strange about bringing your own. Times change.

In 1990, Sheboygan resident, Kathy Alby, started Earthfest to make the public aware of the environment, and show us what we could do to make positive changes—small or large—to make our world a better place in which to live. President Jimmy Carter and my friend in Green Bay, like Kathy, also worked to change the world in a small ways.

Earthfest was originally held at Lakeview Park. In 1992, Kathy moved Earthfest to Vollrath Bowl—the bands played in the bowl; the food, vendors, other musicians, speakers were located in or near the shelter. People wandered up and down the hill, depending on what they wanted to do. The attendance was small. Earthfest competed with other local events like the Coho Derby, or the races at Elkhart Lake. The location of Vollrath Bowl, also, may have deterred people from attending the annual event. A few times Kathy changed the weekend, but then the weather wouldn't cooperate, and it would rain. The first few years I wrote press releases for Kathy, and she had posters posted throughout Sheboygan. The Sheboygan Press wrote articles on Kathy and Earthfest. But the attendance never reached a thousand people. Kathy did not give up.

And then magic happened; Kathy moved Earthfest from Vollrath Bowl to Fountain Park, and the Farmer's Market and Earthfest blended together, each being organic in its own way. Fountain Park was smaller than Vollrath Bowl, which was good: you didn't have to wander up and down the hills, you were right there: you could buy your produce, listen to a band, check out the vendors, and hear a speaker inform the public about alternative forms of energy. And when you wandered around the park, you could always run into a friend. Earthfest is now promoted on billboards, bumper stickers, Facebook, and its own website. The message has gone beyond the word of mouth.

Earthfest is also family-friendly. Craig Virgin, Kathy's husband, helped Kathy run Earthfest. Kathy, though, had other helpers, as well including her children, her sister, her sister's husband; everyone provided a helping hand when Kathy needed it. In the following pages, you'll meet these people, among others. This is a look back at Earthfest, and how it blossomed. Enjoy!

Paul A. Hanson

On August 8, 1991, I "stopped off at Kathy Alby's to give her the press release for the Earthwalk/Earthfest." The press release was in The Sheboygan Press on August 13. I don't know if I attended that year. But I helped Kathy Alby promote the event. The Second Annual Earthfest press release is below:

Second annual Earthfest featured

The second annual Earthfest — A Celebration of Our Existence on Earth, sponsored by Kathy Alby and Maywood Environmental Park, will be held at Lakeview Park (Shooting Park) on Aug. 25 from noon to 9 p.m.

The festivities will begin at 10 a.m., with an earthwalk from North Point Park to Lakeview Park. Walkers will clean up the beach area between the parks. Garbage bags will be provided to the participants. Interested individuals can contact Kathy Alby at 452-3085 for sponsor sheets.

A variety of music — folk, psychedelic, blues, rock 'n roll and original environmental music — will highlight the event. Scheduled bands are Dark Horse from Kohler, Al Haas from Milwaukee, Paul Schlosser from Madison, Grind from Manitowoc, John Prove from Haven and Infinity and Dark Entity from Sheboygan.

Tie-dye shirts and pants, South of the Border clothing, beaded jewelry and other merchandise will be sold by art vendors.

Nature's Best will sell natural foods. Lone Star Mexican and Native American food will also be available, along with Sheboygan's favorite roasted corn, brats, hamburgers, hot dogs and beer.

On August 30, 1992, I wrote in my journal that Kathy Alby had the third annual Earthfest. Kathy Alby changed locations from Lakeview Park to Vollrath Bowl. I took ten photos for Kathy, documenting the event: I have photos of Craig Virgin, Lora Hagen, Diane Bell, and Art Paul Schlosser, whom you'll meet soon.

Kathy Alby and her daughter

August 21, 1994—Kathy Alby and Craig estimate they will lose $1,000 from this year's Earthfest. The event had been rained out twice . . . after the second rain shower the crowd slimmed down to a few.

August 21, 1994—I met a man who built bat houses. Bats are friendly to the environment: I've seen bats eating mosquitos on a hot summer day.

August 24, 1994—At Earthfest, there had been an impromptu singing of "The Wedding Song" from the TV show "Gilligan's Island." The man started singing, "You by my side, that's how I see us, . . ./My secret dreams have all come true-oo." The man stressed the "oo's" in the song. He finished the second and third verse of the song, but when he came to the last verse, he struggled to find the words of the song; seven people helped him; he sang: "I see us now, your hand in my hand,/This is the hour, this is the moment,/And I can hear sweet voices singing, Ave Maria./Ave Maria, Ave Mari-i-a." On "Gilligan's Island," the TV show used "The Wedding," sung by Julie Rogers, and written by Fred Jay and Joaquin Prieto. The song came out in 1964.

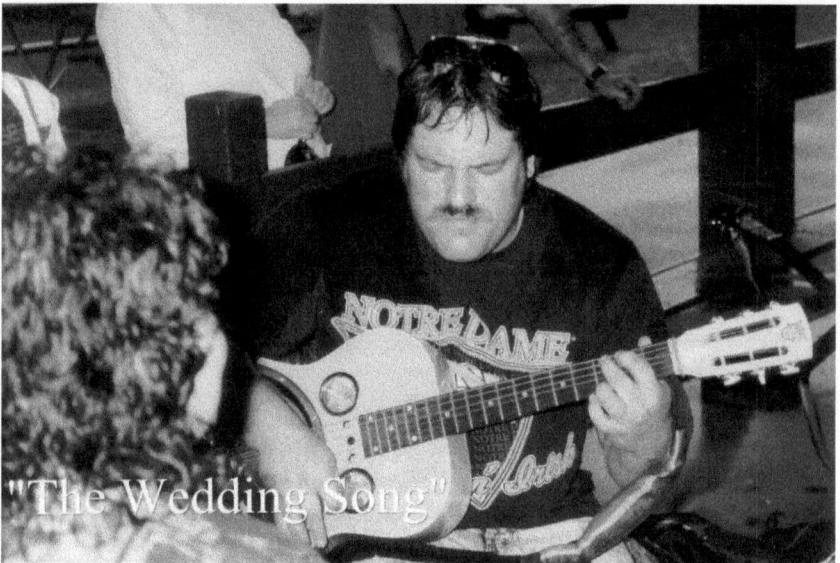

"The Wedding Song"

September 30, 1994—For three years, Pat Ford-Smith has been "Hiccup the Clown." At Earthfest, a man approached her and said, "Hello Hiccup, my name is F—Up." As Pat Ford-Smith, she might have been upset, but as Hiccup the Clown, she continued on to the next child, leaving the man behind her. Later, the man asked her for stickers for his kids.

Hiccup the Clown

1994—You'll see familiar faces in the following pages: some people have returned year after year; while others have only visited Earthfest for one year.

Kathy Alby with her daughter

1994—Scott Hildebrand, Dave Steffen, Keith Abler, and Darryl St. John were the headliner bands. Darryl St. John is from Green Bay, Wisconsin. He sang the blues and rock music solo, and with Dave Steffen.

Darryl St. John

Kristine Pamenter

1994—Kristine Pamenter is a storyteller of fairy tales and folk tales.

1994--Dionne Alby performed that day. She is Kathy Alby's sister.

Dionne Alby

1994--Art Paul Schlosser is a street musician from Madison, Wisconsin. He sang songs from his CDs, My Cat Was Taking a Bath & Dead Skunk Perfume, along with I Want to Be Madonna? He sang the chorus: "I want to be Madonna?/I want to be Madonna?/I want to be Madonna?/How about you?"

Art Paul Schlosser

1994—Jim Baumgart is a member of the Wisconsin State Assembly. He is a Democrat.

Jim Baumgart with his daughter

Kathy Alby

1995—Kathy Alby and Craig Virgin sold beer this year; they attempted to get the "beer crowd."

Craig Virgin

1995—But at the end of the evening, Craig Virgin checked the keg, and found it wasn't empty. At the end of Earthfest, he couldn't find enough people to drink the remaining beer. There weren't enough beer drinkers.

1995—Lora Hagen wore an Earthfest t-shirt. Unlike the beer, if the t-shirts did not sell out, they could always sell them next year. Lora Hagen works for the Sheboygan Area School District.

Lora Hagen and friend

Sheboygan Astronomical Society

1995—Another Earthfest t-shirt. The man, if you noticed, is standing next to a telescope. He is a member of the Sheboygan Astronomical Society, which was established in 1973. They are amateur astronomers who look skyward, to the moon and beyond. They brought tele-scopes and photos of the Milky Way Galaxy.

1995—The Ice Age Trail in Wisconsin is 1200 miles; it starts in
Sturgeon Bay, Wisconsin, and ends in St. Croix Falls, Wisconsin. A
person can hike the whole 1200 miles, or part of the trail. The
Lakeshore Chapter of the Ice Age National Scenic Trail includes
Sheboygan, Manitowoc, Kewaunee, and Door Counties.

Ice Age Park & Trail Exhibit

1995—Dave Steffen played guitar in
Love Society, Sun Blind Lion, and the
Dave Steffen Band. He had record
contracts with Scepter Records, RCA,
and Mercury Records. He was the
opening act for Rush, Boston, Styx,
REO Speedwagon, Huey Lewis & The
News, Santana, and Journey. From
1986 until this year, he lived in San
Francisco. He now lives in Sheboygan
County.

Dave Steffen

1995—Keith Abler played in the
bands Love Society and Phase III,
before releasing his solo album
Pilgrimage in 1975. From 1976
until 1980 he was the vocalist for
Sun Blind Lion.

Keith Abler

1995—In the center of the photograph is Mike Dellger standing next to
his wife. Mike Dellger played drums and wrote lyrics for Love Society
in the 60s and 70s, and then joined Sun Blind Lion from 1976 until
1980.

Mike Dellger

1995—Art Paul Schlosser performed environmental songs, like Jesus Is the Answer: "Jesus is the solution/Even if it's pollution."

Art Paul Schlosser

1995—The musicians performed in Vollrath Bowl, and the audience found a comfortable seat sitting in the bowl, or on the hill.

Vollrath Bowl

1995—While others enjoyed a game of hackeysack .

hackeysack

1995—The Peace Patrol made
sure everything and everyone
stayed in harmony.

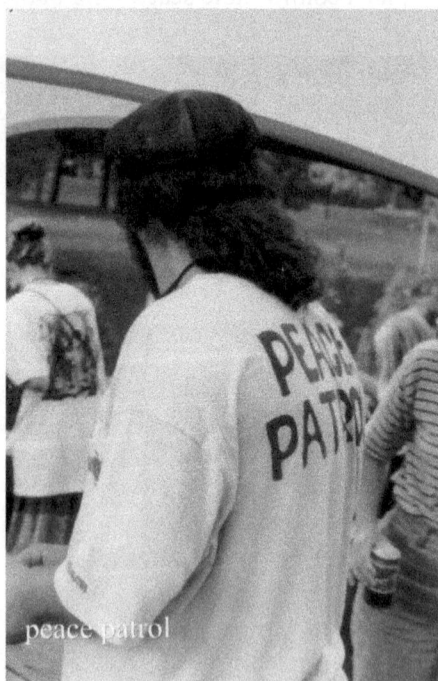

peace patrol

August 17, 1997—Kathy Alby had two photographers taking photos of Earthfest. Last year, Kathy didn't have Earthfest, because she had gotten married. Kathy had her baby with her.

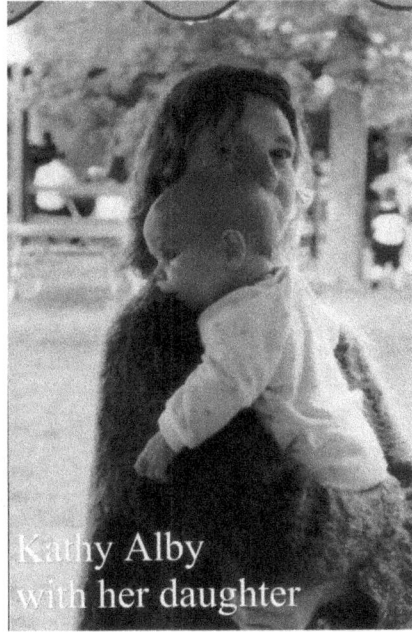

Kathy Alby with her daughter

August 17, 1997—The turnout hadn't been like two years ago. The rain and the Packer game, and the races could have changed people's minds in attending.

Craig Virgin with his daughter

August 17, 1997—The corn was good.

Lora Hagen

1997—Everybody cleared out of Vollrath Bowl when it started to rain, except this lone musician, probably Art Paul Schlosser, and the sound crew, who covered the sound board, and anything electrical.

rain

1997—Kathy Alby attended Sheboygan North High School and graduated in 1976. North High alumni, like Judy Johnston and Jocelyn Ertel,
along with Anna Reif, Karen Spaeth, and others visited Earthfest.

Judy Johnston and Jocelyn Ertel

Diane Bell
with her daughter

1997—Diane Bell, also, attended
North High School.

1997—Art Paul Schlosser displayed a t-shirt he designed. He performed from his CDs, as did Slightly Toasted Band, Sunny Monday, Red House, Polite Virus, MRRR, and Little Rev.

Art Paul Schlosser

1997—At the end of the day, Kathy Alby was able to enjoy that good corn.

Kathy Alby with her daughter

1997---Shahara Falk-LeFay is wearing a circled pentagram. The circle represents eternity, infinity. The five points on the star represent--- earth, air, fire, and water, with the fifth point representing spirit. In early Christianity, the fifth point symbolized Christ.

Shahara Falk-LeFay with her daughter

1997---Eartha the Elf teaches that we must respect our earth, our home. This is our earth, and we must take care of it.

Eartha the elf

August 14, 1999---I wrote a press
release for Kathy for Earthfest.

At right is the 1999 Earthfest flyer.

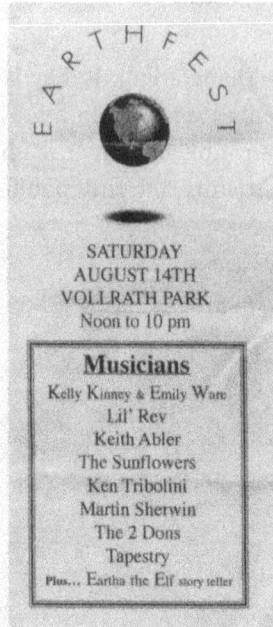

1999---Larry Miller and Dawn Jax Belleau of The Sheboygan Press
wrote about Earthfest; they described the event as "an outdoor
classroom," "to educate, communicate, and celebrate." Dawn Jax Belleau, also, wrote an article on the Butterfly Lady of Parnell, Alice Gil-
lis, who taught children on how to raise butterflies.

2000---Craig Virgin, a.k.a. Craig Wayh, edited, published, and delivered Sheboygan's alternative news magazine, Lakefire, to Plymouth, Sheboygan, Kohler, Sheboygan Falls, and Green Bay. The newspaper has a circulation of 1,800.

Craig Virgin and his daughter

2000---"Movement Creates Change/Change brings about Awareness/Awareness leads to Pure Consciousness/By allowing our minds to open and expand/We enable ourselves to directly experience the/divine Expression within our Bodies." Kathy Alby, from Lakefire March 2000.

Kathy Alby teaches yoga at Mona Elisa Salon

Kathy Alby

2000---Bryon Zimmerman and Jim Wilsing played the bagpipes, which are most known as a Scottish instrument, and are mentioned in Chaucer's Canterbury Tales, written in 1380. But Spain, France, and Italy, also had bagpipes.

Bryon Zimmerman started Gallimore & Zimmerman in 1993, an advertising and design firm. This year he changed the name to ZDO, Zimmerman Design Office.

Besides playing bagpipes, Jim Wilsing handcrafts Native American inspired flutes, which he uses for healing and hospice care.

Byron Zimmerman and Jim Wilsing

2000---Sylvia Bright-Green is a psychic who communicates with the dead, using spirit guides.

Sylvia Bright-Green

2000---Ralph Nader didn't make it to Earthfest, but a representative from the Green Party had campaign materials about Ralph Nader and Winona LaDuke, his running mate. Ralph Nader characterized Al Gore and George W. Bush, the Democrat and Republican nominees, during the election, as "Tweedledee and Tweedledum."

Ralph Nader for President

2000—Mr. and Mrs. Jeff Anderson. Mr. Anderson works for the Sheboygan Area School District. Mrs. Anderson works for the Sheboygan County Humane Society.

Mr. and Mrs. Jeff Anderson

2000—An artist created their own gallery at Vollrath Park.

an artist's gallery

2000—Eartha the Elf performs on the following holidays: earth day, UN Day, and World Environment Day. She talks about the diversity of plants in her folk tales.

eartha the elf

2000—Chris Kuck answered questions on reading labels when grocery shopping; he also explained what was organic, and what was gluten-free.

2000—In Lakefire, March 00, p. 4, The Circle is expanding and our Consciousness is flowing into ever-widening rings of being. It's becoming way too much fun for just a select few to handle. We are opening the doors of opportunity to anyone committed to creating a community of celebration of Dancing and Drumming and Creative Expression. What is not celebrated is soon forgotten. Join us in organizing events that'll Vitalize our community! The Sound Sages, Kathy and Craig.

Kathy Alby & friend

2001—From Lakefire Volume 4, number 4, April 2001.

> **Our grassroots are well embedded ~
> Earthfest** is branching out into boundless
> space and realizing its unlimited potential.
> We are exploring higher ground...
> So all you <u>beautiful</u>, <u>gifted</u> and <u>magnificent</u>
> people ~ (<u>everyone</u>) ~ We know you're out
> there and desire your cooperation.
> Help us bring together ~
>   raise awareness,
>   and celebrate Community!
> **Earthfest** is looking for Musicians -
> Artists - Environmental Organizations -

2002—The vendors were diverse this year: Mobile Mud Coffee House sold coffee from their trailer.

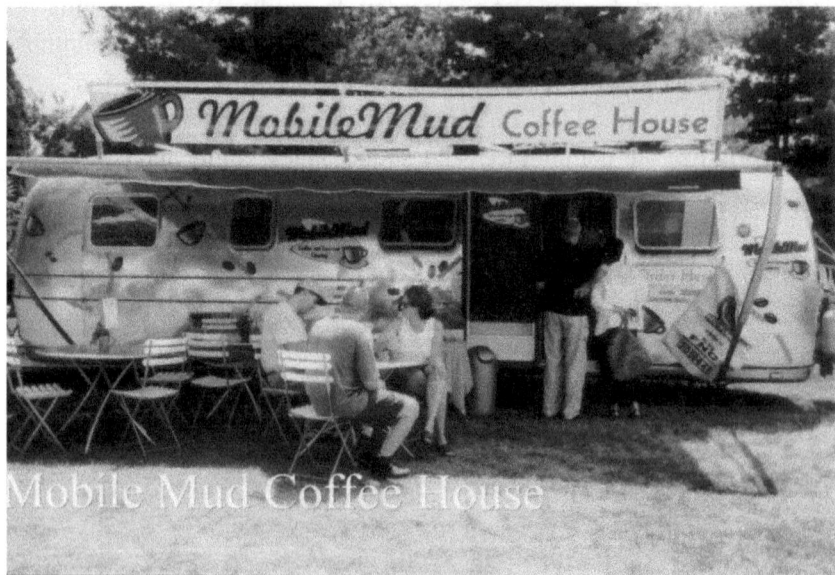

2002—While an artist used the ground as her art gallery.

An Artist

2002—Two men made, demonstrated, and sold their drums.

Two men making drums

2002—SynchroniCity sold books out of boxes.

From the World English Dictionary, the definition of synchronicity is: Noun—An apparently meaningful coincidence in time of two or more similar or identical events that are casually unrelated.

2002—Dear Old Books sold rare and antique books from card tables.

2002—Project Youth had free lemonade. Project Youth assists 16-21 year olds that are homeless find shelter in a safe environment, so that they can complete their high school education.

2002—Craig and Kathy/my brother knows you/drums in hand/by the water blue/guitars and music//Craig and Kathy/I remember your wedding/garments of white/peace and music/in the air//Craig and Kathy/I'm writing again/these words are for you/the ink from my pen/poems and music/stay who you are.

By Java Duke in Lakefire April 2001.

2002—I ain't waiting till I die/I'm gonna go for it now/Yes, there were great people before me/Yes, the saints & sages communed with God/If your religion won't take me there/I will find another path/Let me be judged for that!/It was said that I am the son of God/What then shall I wait for?

By CV Wayh in Lakefire June 01.

Craig Virgin

2002—A young child knows of no separateness/at the age of 3, my daughter Juniper said,/ "I am all names, I am God."/She knows only the Oneness./When she looked into my eyes, she said,/ "Hey, Juniper is in there!"//The separation we feel, is that which we/create ~ that which we think we are./To banish all of that, is to become who we/truly are.

By Kathy Alby, in Lakefire June 01.

Kathy Alby

2002—James "Jim" Young is a Green Party candidate; he is running against James "Jim" Doyle, a Democrat, and Governor Scott McCallum, a Republican, in the Gubernatorial election.

Jim Young and Craig Virgin

2002—Who is Jim Young? He'd like you to know. He was born on June 17, 1960 in Milwaukee, Wisconsin; he received his Bachelor's degree from UW-Milwaukee; he's married; he's a soft-spoken tax assessor from Sun Prairie, Wisconsin. This is his first time running as a gubernatorial candidate, and he's unsure if he'll win. He's running his campaign on a shoestring budget, but he's having fun.

Jim Young campaign employee

2002—Before Judy Stock performed her nose whistle, she informed the audience that she performed this instrument on the "Oprah" Winfrey TV show, on a segment called "Oprah's Funniest Viewers." She reminded the audience that that was her claim to her 15 minutes of fame.

2003—Richard Alby, Kathy Alby's father, died March 6, 2003. He was a World War II US Army Veteran, and he was a teacher at Sheboygan North High School. Richard Alby (September 27, 1925-March 6, 2003).

Remembering Richard Alby: from Paul A. Hanson's Journal of 1976:

April 1, 1976

Mr. Alby, my Psychology teacher, tells stories of his younger days: born in Calcutta, he traveled throughout the world meeting every kind of person imaginable, fought in the war, was in service quite long, he tells of his experiences as a high school teacher. On the weekends, he works in the hardware store at Prange-Way.

May 1, 1976

In Psychology yesterday, Randy Meyer and I went to the library, and then to the radio station. We dedicated "Longfellow Serenade" by Neil Diamond to Richard Alby, because the radio was playing in Psychology.

May 13, 1976

In Psychology, Mr. Alby told the class he wasn't going to be at North High next year: he was going to be in Australia, raising kangaroos on a ranch. Randy Meyer just shook his head, as if saying, "Oh sure, another tall tale."

Richard James Kelt Alby was born in Burlington, Wisconsin on September 27, 1925. He was a winter visitor to Apache Junction, Arizona. He is survived by his wife, Sharon Alby; daughters Victoria Davis, Susan Meyer, Dionne Landgraf, Kathryn Alby and Teresa Alby; stepdaughter Deborah Ernhart; stepsons Duane Alexander and Darren Alexander; sisters Mary Alby and Pat Wisdom; brother Malcolm Alby; seven grandchildren and one great-grandchild.

2003—On August 9th, the location of Earthfest was relocated from Vollrath Park to Fountain Park. People who were at the Farmer's Market could stay and listen to the bands; people who lived in the neighborhood could walk to Earthfest; people that took the city bus could stop at Earthfest, and take a later bus to their destination. Earthfest and the Farmer's Market blended into each other, and a good mix it was.

Kathy Alby

2003—The Society for Creative Anachronism has 19 Kingdoms world-wide. Members of the Society recreate pre-17th century Europe, wearing period clothes, having jousting fights, and eating foods from that time period. Sheboygan County's Shire is Woodlands, Turm an dem See is in the Kingdom of Northshield, which includes North Dakota, South Dakota, Minnesota, Wisconsin, and the Upper Peninsula of Michigan, and it also includes Manitoba and Northwestern Ontario in Canada. Leif Gray Fox and Astrid of the Yellow Rose are the Royalty for Sheboygan County's Shire.

Heather O'Grady and The Society For Creative Anachronism

2003—Art Paul Schlosser was born as Arthur P. Schlosser on January 4, 1960 in Chicago, Illinois. In 2001, Art Paul Schlosser's song "Have a Peanut Butter Sandwich" was played on the "The Dr. Demento Show" four times: on March 25th the song was the top number five song; on June 10th it was number four; on July 8th it was number one; on August 19th, the song dropped down to number three. The song "Have a Peanut Butter Sandwich" was from Art Paul Schlosser's "Reinventing Myself" CD, which was released in the year 2000.

Art Paul Schlosser

2003—Judy Stock and Leigh Robert will open a coffeehouse, Wonderful World, on Michigan Avenue in October 2003; they named the business after Louis Armstrong's song of the same name. The song was written by George David Weiss, George Douglas, and Bob Thiele. "I see trees of green, red roses, too,/I see them bloom, for me and you/And I think to myself/What a wonderful world."

Judy Stock

2003—Shahara Falk-LeFay wrote a poem called "We," which was based on the pentagram; she incorporated water, wind, earth, fire, and the spirit. Her poem appeared in the March 00 Lakefire. She wrote the poem in April 1998.

Shahara Falk-LeFay and her daughter

2003—An artist made didgeridoos, which is an Australian Aboriginal wind instrument. A woman is trying the instrument. In the Aboriginal culture, she would not be allowed to do this. Only men were allowed to play the instrument.

a woman playing a didgeridoo

2003---Craig Virgin was cooking brats earlier; now, he's selling them.

Craig Virgin with a customer

August 12, 2003—At the Fountain Park church service (on Sunday August 10th), the minister told the congregation "that a pagan festival happened the day before on Saturday." The minister never attended Earthfest, so how could he speak as he did. Kathy Alby was surprised to hear the news.

Dionne Alby with Craig Virgin

2004—Motherfest, a fundraiser for Earthfest, was held on Mother's Day, May 9th, at the Quarryview Park Shelter in Sheboygan, Wisconsin. After the opening ceremony, Dionne Alby performed, with Craig Virgin on the drum. Other performers were Uncle Turk, Kristine Wildflower, Mary Jo Zagozen, The New Women's Music Ensemble, Dustin Alexandroni, Heavy Velvet, Matemo Saike, Karen Howland, with drumming ending the evening.

Banjo Maker--Mike Gregory

2004—Banjo Maker Mike can make, repair, or remodel a banjo. He can also make a banjo with whatever he can find around the house. He was born Mike Gregory in 1945, and he is the fifth of eleven chidren. He founded the Grumpystiltskyn Jug Band. He'll be glad to sing you a song using his banjo.

2004—An old proverb—"Patience is a flower that grows not in everyone's garden." Kristine Wildflower entertained and educated the audience on Wisconsin wildflowers and weeds. Two years ago, Kurt Rentmeester wrote an article for the Sheboygan Press on the 11th annual Earthfest fundraiser, which was held at the Fieldhouse at Kiwanis Park. Visitors to the event were trying to reconnect with their spirituality, because of the tragedy on September 11th at the World Trade Center and the Pentagon. Kristine Wildflower, a.k.a. Kristine Pamenter, a member of the Baha'i faith, did not agree with individuals that embraced nationalism through their religious beliefs. She believed that "God is a loving, kind, compassionate God."

Kristine Wildflower

2004—At 3pm, the New Women's Music Ensemble was scheduled to perform. Most people didn't know what to expect from four women that called themselves a Music Ensemble. Most people started wandering around the Quarryview Park Shelter, getting something to eat, or checking out the vendors. But when the music started playing, they wandered right back to the stage. The four women became "one" with their instruments and voices, and the audience became "one" with them. The four women may have come in to Earthfest as the New Women's Music Ensemble, but they left as DivaNation.

2004—Children's artwork adorned the Quarryview Park Shelter wall.

2004—Sylvia Bright-Green is taking a break from doing her readings; she is getting a massage. She has been a correspondent for the Green Bay Press Gazette, the Sheboygan Press, the Milwaukee Journal, and she has been a columnist for Grandparenting Magazine and the Depot Dispatch.

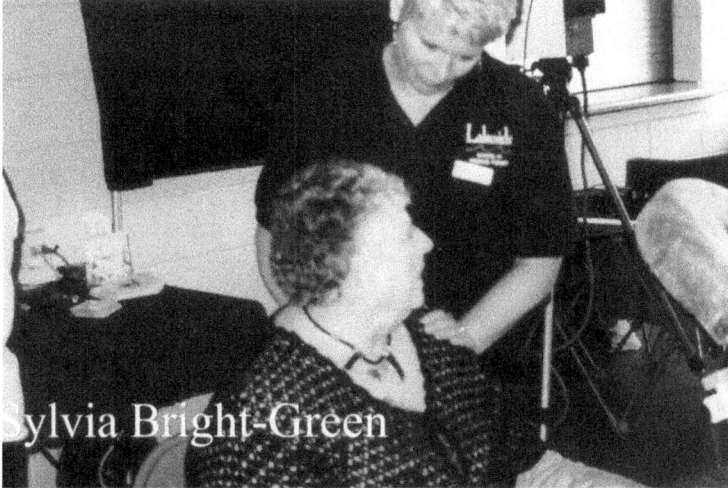

Sylvia Bright-Green

2004—Craig Virgin asked for volunteers to clean the Quarry.

cleaning the Quarry

2004—The kitchen is closed. Mary Denning and Lora Hagen have closed and cleaned the kitchen. Mary Denning and Lora Hagen work the Sheboygan Area School District and Craig Virgin works at the Friendship House.

Mary Denning, Lora Hagen, Craig Virgin

2004—Kathy Alby was 16 years old when she learned yoga; at 19, she opened a health food store called Simply Nature; she ran the store by herself, until her mother helped her. The store was open for ten years. She has four daughters. And she has been married for 17 years to Craig Virgin. She is a massage therapist at Lighthouse Therapy Services, where she also teaches yoga. She, also, organizes drum circles through-out the community. She is the founder and coordinator of Motherfest and Earthfest.

Kathy Alby

2004—Craig Virgin started the drum circle at 8pm; they will perform for an hour, ending the Motherfest festivities for the year.

Craig Virgin, my 1st drum circle

2004—The musical line-up for Earthfest this year is Jim Wilsing, Diva-Nation, Uncle Turk, Eartha the Elf, Matemo Saike, Karen Howland, Uriah Scott, Heavy Velvet, Tribolini, Slacker, and the OM Drum Rhythms.

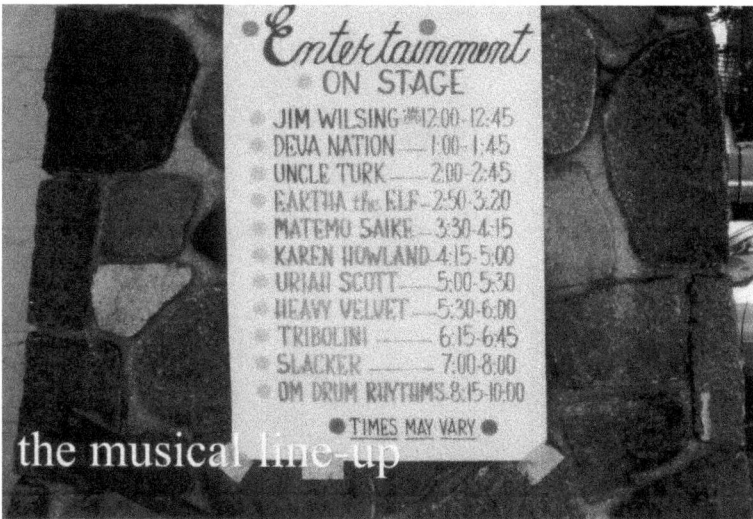

the musical line-up

2004—Matemo Saike, which means "Going to Heaven," and Cole Phillips are listening to DivaNation.

Matemo Saike and Cole Phillips

2004—The people. When Earthfest moved from Vollrath Park to Fountain Park, the people found the family-friendly, eco-friendly event.

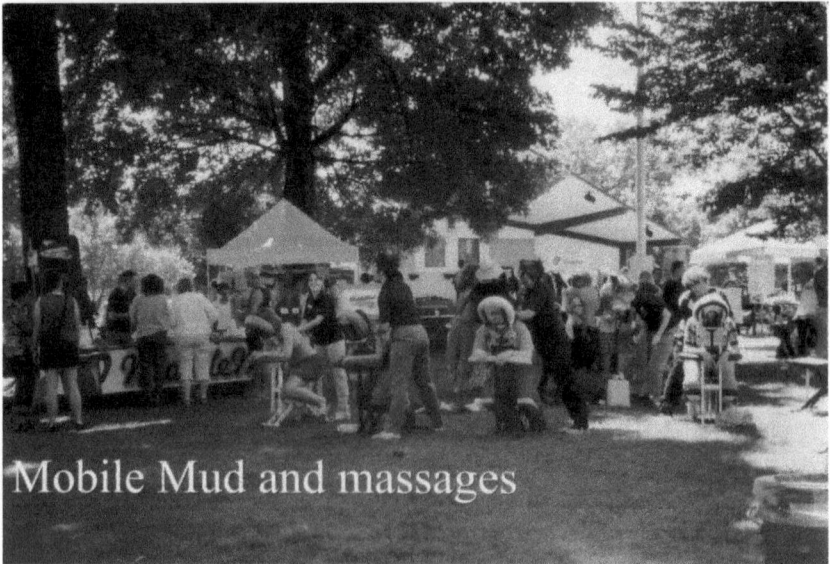

Mobile Mud and massages

2004—Chris Kuck owned a business on Eighth Street called Outside the Box, a gallery of his artwork, and other people locally. He also sold retro candy, and other retro products. He designed the Earthfest poster, and gave it to Kathy Alby.

Chris Kuck's earthfest poster

2004—Kathy Alby is a registered Yoga Teacher with Yoga Alliance. The Yoga Alliance is a non-profit organization, which recognizes yoga teachers and schools that follow a minimum of standards.

Kathy Alby

2004—Mary Denning works for the Sheboygan Area School District.

2004—Craig Virgin graduated from Sheboygan North High School in 1983.

2004—Uriah Scott performed onstage, along with

2004—Shannon Hoitink.

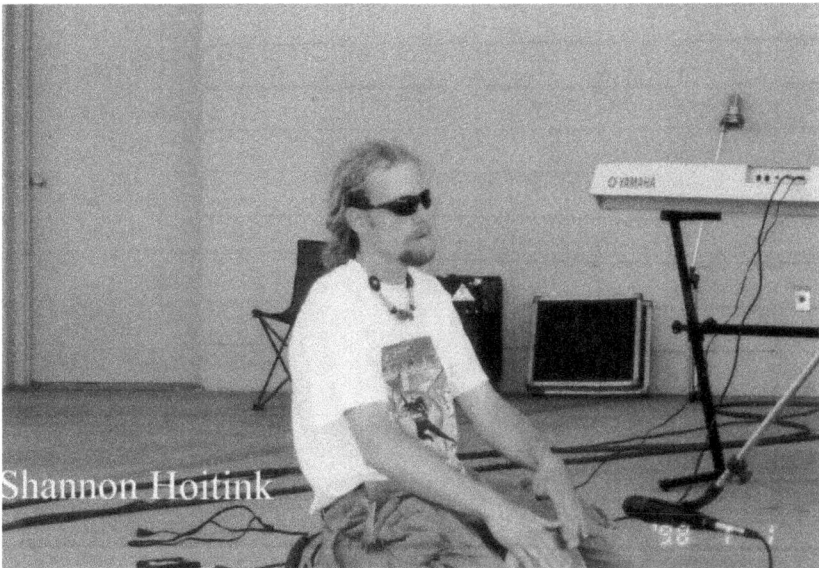

2004—Heavy Velvet performed.

2004—At Earthfest, you could see men wearing dresses; they started their own club locally.

2004—Uncle Turk is relaxing after his performance.

Uncle Turk

2004—Tribolini performed from their CDs, Worlds Within (1994) and Lifetimes Ago (2002). Ken Tribolini started Whispering Hills Music in 1991. It is located on 40 acres of land in Kiel, Wisconsin.

Tribolini

2004—Uncle Turk and Cole Phillips, along with Heavy Velvet, Kristine Pamenter, and others participated in the drum circle.

Uncle Turk and Cole Phillips

2005—Shannon Hoitink opened Glass Illusions, LLC on June 20, 2005. Shannon is a glass blower who creates modern art. His studio is located on Indiana Avenue in Sheboygan.

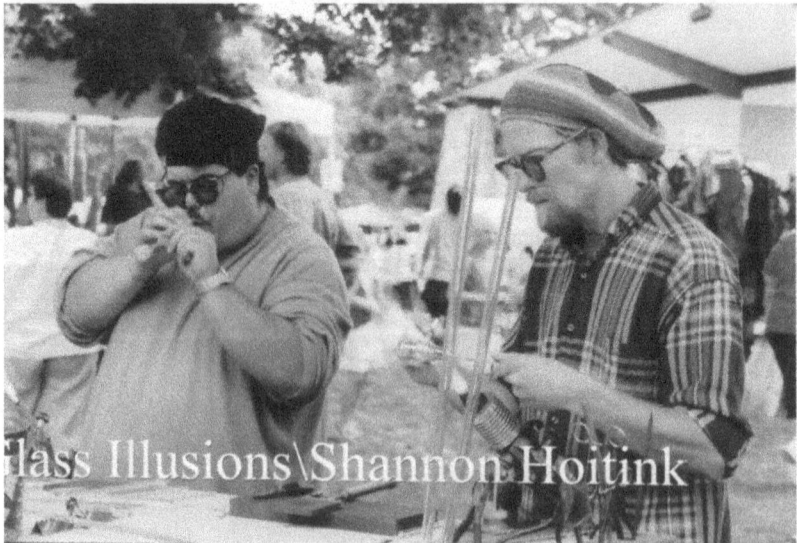

Glass Illusions\Shannon Hoitink

2005—On March 15, 1972, a Wednesday, at 3:30PM, the Girl Scout Troop 324 planned on performing the play, "The Mount Vernon Cricket" at the Mead Library. The play is about a footstool that has the initials "G.W." printed on it. And those initials must stand for George Washington. Anyone that sits on the stool must tell the truth. Kathy Alby, Vicki Holt, Debbie Johnson, Lois Reinholtz, Linda Reinholtz, Janet Rusch, Judy Rusch, and Ruth Schmitt were the performers, and Mrs. Richard Alby was the troop leader.

2005—The Pain Buddy: from the Bing dictionary: pain: emotional distress: severe emotional or mental distress; buddy: friend: a good friend, coworker, companion, or partner.

2005—Masks: from the Bing dictionary; concealing thing; something that conceals or disguises something else, such as true motives or feelings.

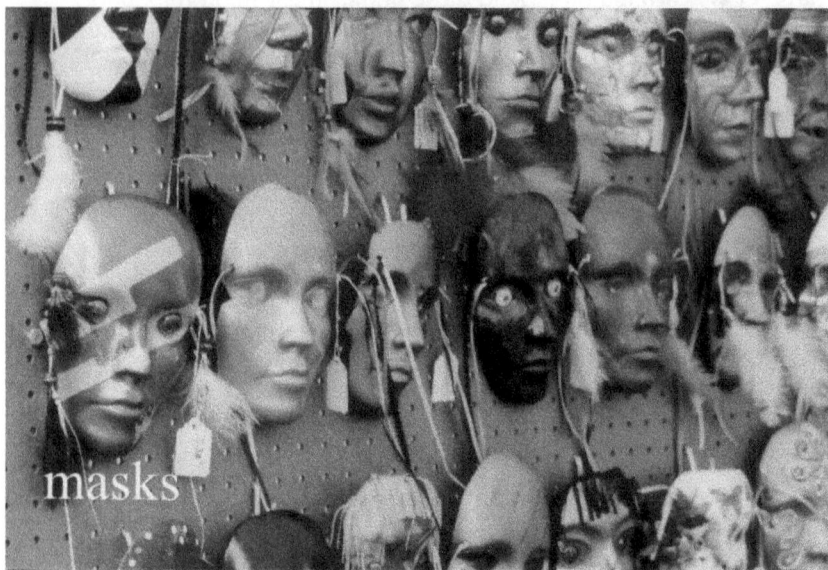

2005---Greeting cards designed by Chris Kuck: he is an artist, who likes Terry Bozzio, drums, and graphic design.

2005---A yoga teacher teaching young girls yoga. Yoga is a Hindu discipline which promotes spirituality with a supreme being through breathing exercises and postures.

2005—Chris Kuck on drums.

2005—In the *Sheboygan Press* on May 1, 1973, Janet Rusch, Judy Rusch, Vicki Holt, Ruth Schmitt, Debbie Johnson, Lois Reinholtz, Kathy Alby, and Linda Reinholtz of Girl Scout Troop 324 became First Class Scouts. Their community projects included surveying poorly lighted areas of Sheboygan, and presenting the information to the common council; distributing REACH posters, along with other activities. The troop hiked 50 miles to attend Summerfest. To fund the awards dinner, the girl scouts sold cookies, and had a paper drive. The parents of the scouts attended the dinner at Johnnie's Supper Club.

Kathy Alby

2005—Craig Daven Virgin and Kathryn J. Alby were married on January 28, 1996.

Craig Virgin

2005—A drum circle ended the evening, with the assistance of the Oshkosh Rhythm Section and Robin Cardell: Robin would let each individual express himself through the drum; he approached each individual, and asked him or her to play their instrument, which that individual did; then each individual contributed, one by one, to the entire circle of drums.

Oshkosh Rhythm Section

2005—And as the evening got darker, the drums sounded louder, echoing throughout the neighborhood. Each individual realized their individual role in the drum circle, but he also realized how his individual drum beat contributed to the whole. Robin Cardell had the group drum a finale, and he took his bow for the evening. If someone felt like a stranger within the group, by the end of the evening, he felt like he was one with the group. Drugs were not needed for this kind of high: the lake breeze, the drumming, it all contributed to the high.

Robin Cardell

2006—what is a tree hugger? Words related to tree hugging are vegan, vegetarian, hippie, environmentalist, flower child. The tree hugger protects the environment, especially trees. If you've forgotten, trees give humans oxygen, and humans give trees carbon dioxide. There is a connection between humans and trees.

2006—Chris Kuck and Karen Howland performing on stage. Karen Howland is a poet, and a musician.

2006—Kathy Alby is wearing a tie-dye shirt, which have been associated with hippies. Hippies became famous when they attended Woodstock in Bethel, New York on Max Yasgur's farm on August 15-18, 1969. Richie Havens, Arlo Guthrie, Joan Baez, Santana, Canned Heat, Grateful Dead, Janis Joplin, Sly & the Family Stone, The Who, Jefferson Airplane, and others performed that day. Kathy Alby was 11 years old in 1969. She has seen the Grateful Dead, though.

2006—John "Little John" Holzwart is a Traditional Broom Maker: he makes functional, but playful brooms. Chris Kuck you've met. Ellen Crow has studied yoga, Middle Eastern dance, African dnce, ballet, and tai chi. She is a certified yoga teacher.

"Little John," Chris Kuck, Ellen Crow

2006—Full Freedom International sells a gasoline additive which will boost your gas mileage.

Full Freedom International

2006—Wendy Honold is a poet, Shannon Hoitink, and Chris Kuck you've met.

Wendy Honold, Shannon Hoitink, Chris Kuck

2006—Mickey Hart, a drummer from the Grateful Dead, spoke before the United States Senate Special Committee on Aging in 1991: he stated that there is equality in a drum circle: there is no head, there is no tail. The objective of the drum circle is to share rhythm, to "get in tune with each other and themselves," forming a new collective voice. Source: Wikipedia "The Drum Circle."

Drum Circles

2006—Chris Kuck made a new Earthfest banner for the 2006 Earthfest event.

Chris Kuck's earthfest banner

2006—"To know how to spend your money, have a talk with your purse."—unknown author

a purse vendor

2006—If you decide to make your own incense, you'll need the following: an incense recipe, fresh natural aromatic ingredients, a grinder, measuring devices, and jars for storage.

an incense vendor

2006—knitting and crocheting; they may look similar, but they are actually different: crocheting uses one hook needle, and one loop is made at a time, creating a chain; knitting uses two needles with no hooks;

crocheting and knitting

2006—The musical line-up included:

Judy Stock

Roger Chrapla

Cayuse Cowboys--Cedar Grove Slim played guitar, Silver Dollar Jim played violin, and Miss Kate played bass; they sang songs of the Silver Screen Cowboys; a cayuse is a small native American pony used by cowboys.

Karen Howland—attended Marquette University, the UW-Milwaukee, and the Conservatory of Music.

DivaNation with Celia—Celia's recorded Breathe in 2003.

Mary Bue—is from Duluth, Minnnesota. In 2001 she recorded Where the Monarchs Circled, and in 2003, East to the Sea.

Michael Ammons—sings solo, and also with the Water Street Hot Shots.

Liv'Rev—"I'm a deep-rooted musician, songwriter, instrumentalist, storyteller, historian, interpreter of traditional Americana music and culture."

Uncle Turk

Jason Moon—is a Vietnam vet who uses music to heal: in 1997 he released Naked Under All These Clothes.

Jason Kaufman

Turkish Blend

Babar

The Brimleys—started in 2005: they play blues, funk, punk, and blue grass. Rob Shively, Ric Bourbonais, Brandon Colella, Nate Ford, and Mickey Kennedy are the band members.

Cedarwell—Eric Neave, Jared Beckman, and Jeff Patlin: Play the Moon came out in 2002, and End of All the Latest Trends came out in 2004.

2006—Uriah Scott manned the soundboard.

2006—Dr. Dionne Alby Landgraf, and her husband Mark Landgraf; they are both visual artists. Dr. Dionne Alby Landgraf has a B.A. from Rutgers University, an M.F.A. from Northern Illinois University and a Ph.D. from the University of Wisconsin-Madison. She is an Associate Professor of Art and Director of Art Education at Silver Lake College in Manitowoc.

2006—Karen Howland performs for children at the children's stage, while Chris Kuck looks on.

Karen Howland

2006—Nelson Eisman is the Green Party's candidate for Governor of Wisconsin. Ed Thompson, Tommy Thompson's brother, told Nelson Eisman that "you're the only one in this race talking common sense." Jim Doyle and Mark Green are running against him, and Nelson Eisman said, "If you're for the lesser of two evils, what you're voting for is at the end of the sentence—evil." "Democracy is about finding a candidate that resonates with you."

Quotes from "Green Party Candidate Looking for Respect," The Badger Herald, September 19, 2006, except Ed Thompson's quote, which was in Steve Herrick-Eisman Gives Voters a Choice, October 30, 2006.

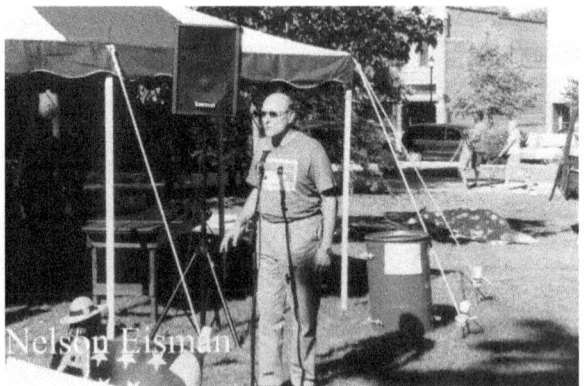

Nelson Eisman

2006—Craig Virgin reciting the Pledge of Allegiance—"I Pledge Allegiance to the flag of the United States and to the Republic for which it stands, one Nation under God, indivisible, with Liberty and Justice for all."

Craig Virgin

Sue Alby-Meyer

2006—Sue Alby-Meyer, Kathy Alby's sister. Sue Alby graduated from Sheboygan North High School in 1972; Dionne Alby graduated from Sheboygan North High School in 1973.

2006—Kathy Alby, Craig Virgin, and Whitney Stefano. Whitney Viglietti, along with her husband, Stefano Viglietti, owns and operates four restaurants in Sheboygan; they are Trattoria Stefano, Il Ritrovo, Field to Fork, and Duke of Devon.

Kathy Alby, Whitney Stefano, Craig Virgin

2006—The beverage station—available to drink—water and organic soda, Blue Sky.

the beverage station

Linda Conroy

2006—Linda Conroy is a Bioregional herbalist, Wild, Whole, and Local Food Aficionado, Home Cheese Maker, and all around Wise Woman. She owns Moonwise Herbs & Brooms.

2006—At Moonwise Herbs & Brooms, Linda Conroy offers classes and workshops on identifying wild herbs and plants, and what they are best used for---medicine or food. She also sells brooms that can decorate a wall, or can be used for sweeping.

Moonwise Herbs

2006—Recycling bins labeled paper or mixed recycling could be found throughout Fountain Park.

recycling

Mixed Recycling

2006—Liana J. Sittman, Kathy Alby's daughter.

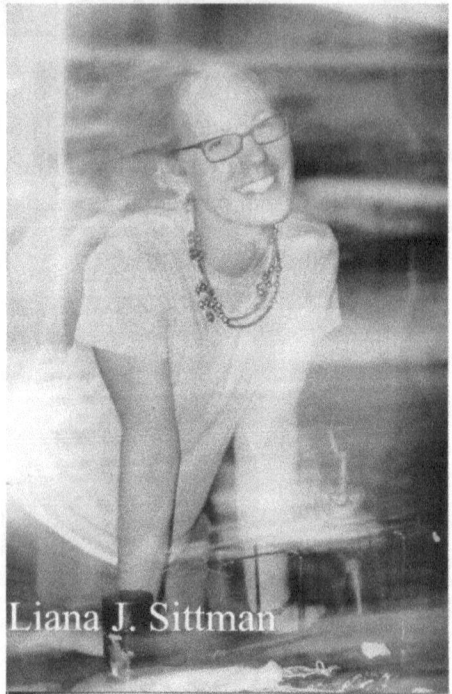

Liana J. Sittman

2007—In July 2007, on the Plant Based People website, an individual wrote, "First local event I know of that is offering veggie anything (wraps/burgers). Keep in mind this area is the self-proclaimed Bratwurst capital of the world. So this is BIG for our little town."

2007—The Sierra Club, a grassroots environmental organization, was founded in 1892 by John Muir (1838-1914), a naturalist and conservationist. John Muir wrote the following, "The battle we have fought, and are still fighting for the forests is a part of the eternal conflict between right and wrong, and we cannot expect to see the end of it. . . . So we must count on watching and striving for these trees, and should always be glad to find anything so surely good and noble to strive for."

2007—Family Farmer Grilled Cheese—when making grilled cheese sandwiches, you can use sliced apples, tomatoes, bacon, or you can also change the cheese—pepper jack, or combine two cheeses together—sharp cheddar with Swiss cheese.

2007—Peace Action Wisconsin is the largest grassroots peace network in the United States.

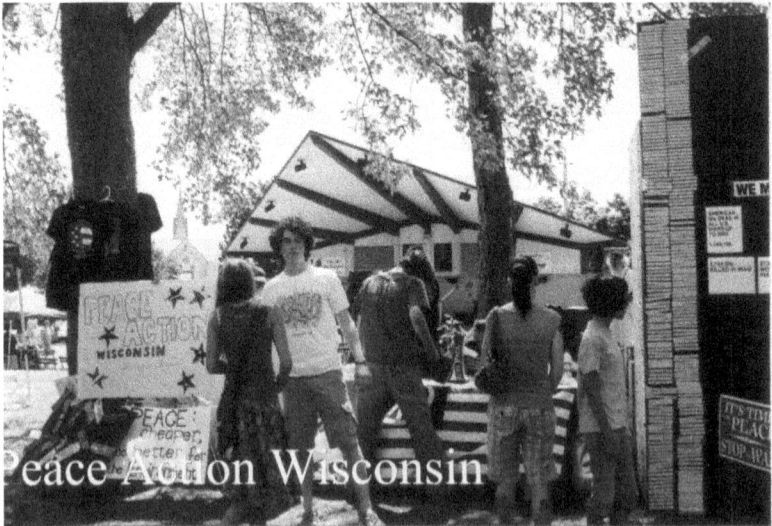

2007—The Farmer's Market and Earthfest complimented each other. People could buy their produce, pies, or canned goods, and then attend Earthfest. Once a month, The Farmer's Market sells crafts.

crafts at the farmer's market

2007—Crawford Smith is a retired Research & Development Specialist from Vinyl Plastics (VPI), and Pat Ford-Smith owns Happy Times Costumes N'More; she is also known as Hiccup the Clown, and other singing telegram characters; she is also a religious instructor with Grace Episcopal Church.

Crawford Smith & Pat Ford-Smith

2007—Kathy Alby is doing a live "videotaped" interview with the Sheboygan Press.

2007—Don Reetz, Jr. is the man who made the bat houses in 1994.

2007—The Members of Peace Action Wisconsin have arrested George W. Bush (43rd President, elected 2001 to the present), Dick Cheney (46th Vice President of the United States, elected 2001 to the present), Donald Rumsfeld (Secretary of Defense, 1975-1977, and 2001 to the present), and Condoleeza Rice, (Secretary of State from 2005 to the present) for starting the wars in Iraq and Afghanistan.

2007—a Hmong vendor. The Hmong came to Wisconsin in 1975, especially men that were associated with General Vang Pao's Secret Army, who assisted the United States during the Vietnam War.

2007—Craig Virgin hosts the open mike at Paradigm Café on North Eighth Street in Sheboygan, Wisconsin.

Craig Virgin

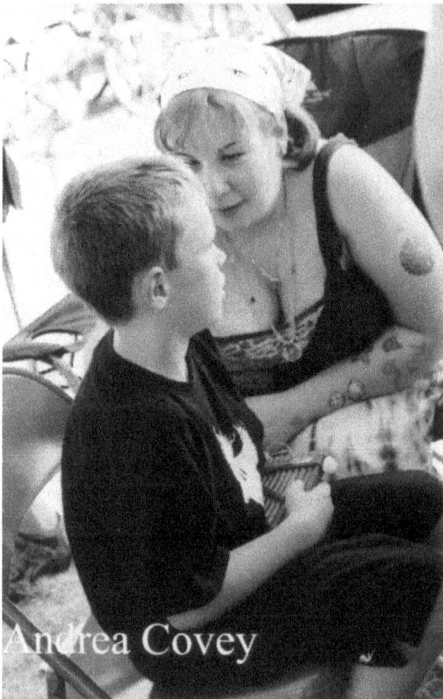

Andrea Covey

2007—Andrea Covey joined the Earthfest committee in 2007. She wanted to add a children's area to Earthfest. Here she is face painting a child.

2007—Sequoia Virgin is Kathy Alby's daughter. Sequoia Virgin sings the blues.

Sequoia Virgin

Earthfest Speakers

11:00 am	The Urban Garden Vickie Hall, Friends of Sheboygan's Parks
11:30 am	Native Plant Landscaping Joe Majerus, Landmark Landscape
12:00 pm	Sustainable Transportation Aaron Brault, Non-Motorized Transportation Program
12:30 pm	Herbal Remedies for Sustainability Linda Conroy, Moonwise Herbs
1:00 pm	Beyond Organic Stefano Viglietti, Field to Fork and Grocery
1:30 pm	Preserving Working Lands Rolf Johnson, Glacial Lakes Conservancy

Special Guest!

2:00 pm	Urban Farming & Community Food Centers Will Allen, Growing Power

Introduction by Fred Depies, Glacierland RC&D

Will Allen is the founder of Growing Power Inc. and is a pioneer in organic and sustainable farming methods in an urban and rural setting. Mr. Allen is also an educator and international lecturer on aquaponics, aquaculture, beekeeping, animal husbandry, biological worm growing, year-round growing of greens in cold-weather climates.

2:45 pm	Creating Food Councils Speaker Change: Will Allen will speak for Erica Allen
3:30 pm	Fair and Free Trade John Peck, Family Farm Defenders
4:00 pm	Renewable Energy Advocacy Jennifer Eigenberger, LTC Solar & Wind Power Instructor
4:30 pm	Hot and Cold Effects on Food Production Steve Klug, Sustainability

2007—When Kathy Alby started Earthfest, she would invite speakers to provide information on certain topics; in 2007, the speaker list included Vickie Hall who talked about the Urban Garden; Aaron Brault who talked about Sustainable Transportation; Linda Conroy on Herbal Remedies; Stefano Viglietti on Beyond Organic; Will Allen on Urban Farming; John Peck on Fair and Free Trade and Jennifer Eigenberger on Renewable Energy Advocacy.

2007—The bellydancers' audience waited patiently for the bellydancers.

2007—The bellydancers arrived. Some of the women used bellydancing as a weight-loss program, while others wanted to lose weight after having a baby.

2007—Kathy Alby was able to take a break and watch the bellydancers.

2008—In Janet Ortegon's Sheboygan Press article on Earthfest, "Sustainable Living: Earth Fest Promotes Community Spirit," which came out on August 18, 2008, Kathy Alby said, "Being green is hip and trendy. We are moving toward sustainable living because we have to."

2008—Earthfest has grown. According to Haley Kosup-Kennedy in the Sheboygan Press "Sustainable Living" article, she said, "It's definitely expanded a lot. The popularity of it has definitely grown. . . . I love the whole atmosphere. I'm very much a hippie fanatic. I admire the life-style. I've always wanted to live in the 70s. I'm seeing a lot of cool things."

the people

2008—Cole Phillips is an arborist for Arborist Arts, a landscaping company in Sheboygan, Wisconsin.

Cole Phillips

2008—Craig Virgin is listening to his daughter Sequoia Virgin perform on stage, while talking to two patrons of Earthfest. A list of sponsors is listed on a banner in back of Craig.

2008—Lakeshore Technical College (LTC) teaches students on wind energy technology. A student can learn how to install, service, and repair wind turbine components. Wind turbines are used to generate electricity. And are an alternative to fossil fuels, such as coal or oil.

2008—Even though Earthfest grew, grassroots vendors (not an established business) sold their merchandise.

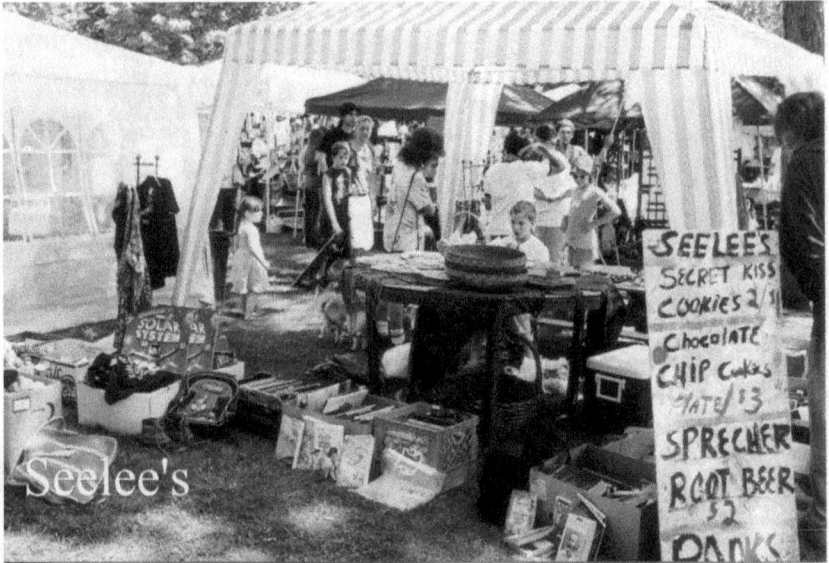

Seelee's

2008—Jim Baumgart with his daughter. Jim Baumgart was a Wisconsin State Assemblyman from 1990-1996, in the Wisconsin State Senate from 1998-2002, and is a Sheboygan County Board Member from 2004 to the present. He also writes "Crosstrails" in The Shoreline Chronicle.

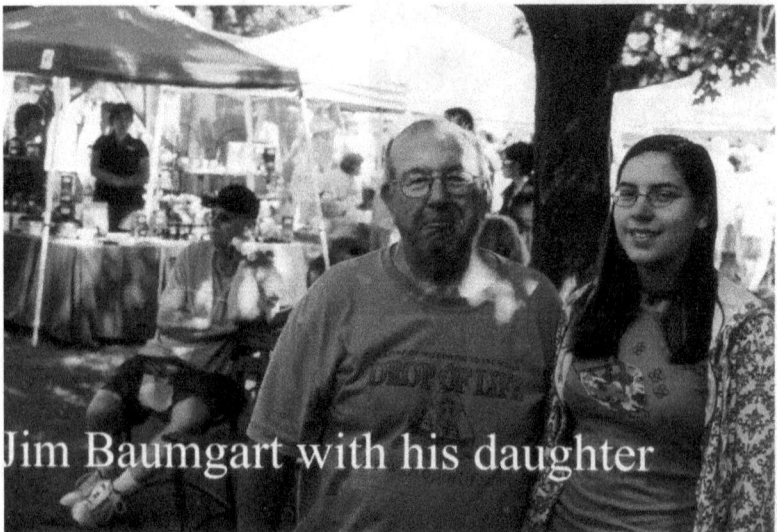

Jim Baumgart with his daughter

2008—Kathy Alby performed with her daughter, Sequoia Virgin.

2008—The speakers this year spoke from the Main Stage, instead of the Speakers' Tent. Mark Winne is talking about community food systems and food policy: he organized a breakfast program for low-income children in Maine.

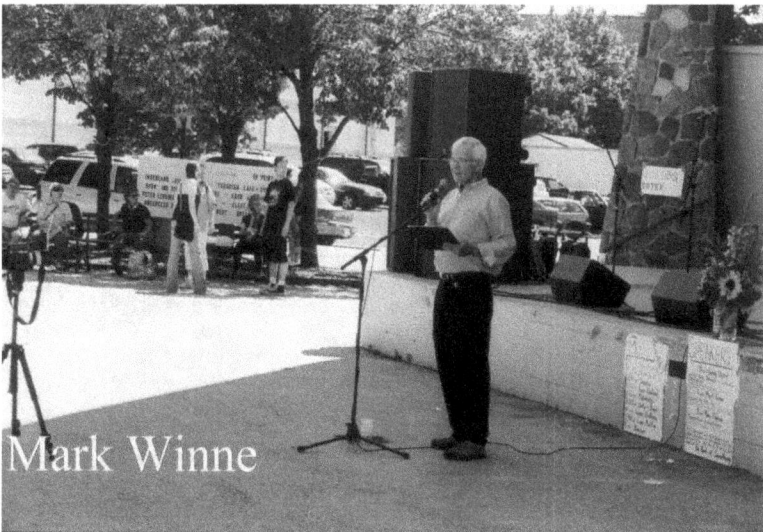

2008—Four children spontaneously brought the sheet onto the stage, and started performing with it.

children performing

2008—The bellydancers' audience continued to increase.

the bellydancer's audience

2008—During Earthfest, Craig Virgin and Kathy Alby were rarely seen together, because Kathy could be found selling tickets, and Craig would be helping making brats and hamburgers.

Craig Virgin and Kathy Alby

2008—Paradigm Coffee & Music is a café located on North 8th Street in Sheboygan, Wisconsin; they use local food suppliers like Colectivo Coffee Roaster, Rishi Tea Company, and Omanhenee Cocoa Bean Company from Milwaukee, Wisconsin, and City Bakery, The She-boygan's Farmer Market and Goodside Grocery from Sheboygan, Wis-consin.

Paradigm Cafe

2008—Earthfest had grown: there was music, speakers, an event tent, which featured demonstrations on glass blowing, Latin dance, on drumming, belly dancing, and yoga; in the kids corner, there was storytelling, face painting, crafting and games; in the attractions, there was massage therapy, earth friendly vendors and a drum circle.

2008—Andrea Covey changed the Happy Hour to Hippy Hour.

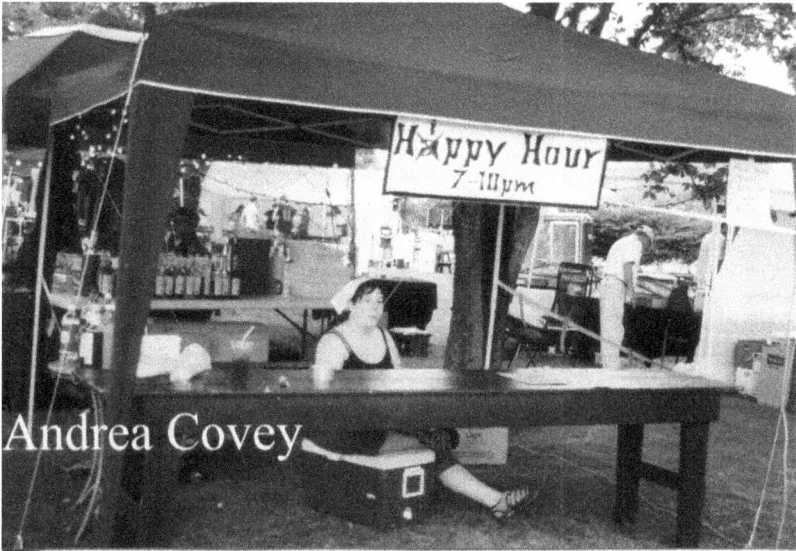

2008—On August 1, 2009, Kathy Alby and friends advertised Earthfest in the Bratwurst Day Parade.

2009—The vendors are setting up their tents, and what's inside their tents. Earthfest will open in a few hours.

August 15, 2009

2009—The man is setting up the food stand: he is moving a bag of corn closer to the grill.

food preparation

2009—Craig Virgin and Tom Mayer are talking with a woman/
volunteer before Earthfest starts; they are very relaxed.

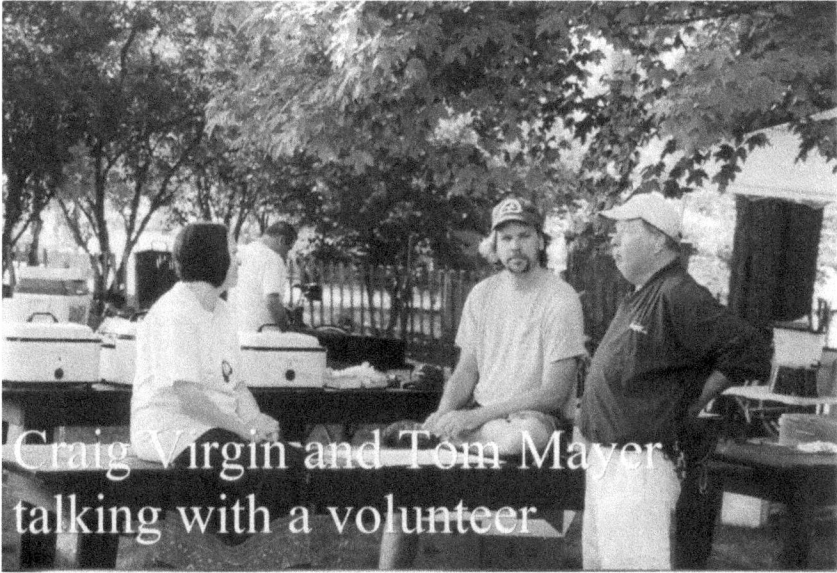

Craig Virgin and Tom Mayer
talking with a volunteer

2009—A bike corral was added to Earthfest; visitors were encouraged
to bike to Fountain Park, and leave their bike in the corral, which was
protected by a staff person.

a bike corral

2009—Bookworm Gardens started as a dream for Sandy Livermore: she envisioned a garden where children could explore literature, and be surrounded by the story: if the child read "The Three Little Pigs," the child would see the three houses mentioned in the story.

Bookworm Gardens

2009—A man is explaining to the woman from Bookworm Gardens, how a hydro-garden works: he raised his plants using water, instead of soil.

a hydro-garden

2009—Toni Mattern is holding the tambourine. She works for the SASD. She is standing in front a van that has a sign in its window: No Parking/Glass Blower Parking Only.

2009—A mother and her child are enjoying their dip into the water at Fountain Park.

2009—Kate Krause, from Paradigm Coffee & Music, is biking people around the park.

2009--These girls are playing with the hula hoops. The hula hoop was invented in 1958 by Arthur K. Melin and Richard Knerr. A hula hoop can be twirled around a waist, a neck, an arm or a leg.

2009—A tight-rope walker set up his rope and safety rope.

tight rope walking

2009—The man is teaching a girl how to walk on the tight-rope. She is also being assisted by the father to maintain her balance.

teaching tight rope walking

New to Earthfest this year was the Coffeehouse, where Don Burhop, and many familiar names over the years performed. Also, Beverly Smith from De Pere, Wisconsin, performed "Rachel Carson: A Voice for the Earth." Rachel Carson wrote Silent Spring, which came out in 1962. Silent Spring documents the use of DDT and other pesticides, and the environmental damage done to humans and wildlife.

Kathy Alby and Ron Mulder

2010—A caterpillar turns into a butterfly. For Earthfest's 20th anniversary, it will be held on two days, August 20th and 21st, and this year's theme is "Back to Our Roots." Earthfest started out like a caterpillar, inching along, until . . . in the Environmental Groups & Projects Resource Guide, for Sheboygan and Sheboygan County, (data collected 2009, expanded and updated 2010), Earthfest is listed on page 6 as a two day event with an environmental theme; guest speakers; panel discussions; ecological exhibits; earth-friendly booths; hot/cold food; musical performers; a coffeehouse-style stage; kids activity center; drum circle; farmers market on Saturdays; Earthfest donates money raised to local non-profit environmental groups and organizations . . . the caterpillar turned into a butterfly.

2010—Mary L. Thorne is the Caterpillar Caregiver, who attends Earth-fest annually. She brings her caterpillars, and she teaches people on "How to Raise a Monarch Butterfly." When the monarch butterfly emerges from its chrysalis, there is excitement; a new life is borne.

a monarch butterfly

2010—Three women were practicing yoga in the Earthfest Yoga Space; they are doing Yin/Restorative Yoga. Hatha Yoga will be done later today, and tomorrow, Parent & Child Yoga is planned, along with Family Yoga and Teen Yoga.

yoga in the park

2010—This woman made costumes for people who participated in medieval events with The Society for Creative Anachronism. She is dressed like a Queen.

a dressmaker

2010—Pop's Corn moved into Fountain Park. He sells freshly squeezed lemonade, water, cotton candy, pretzels, and of course pop-corn.

Pop's Corn

2010—The Spotlight Theater performed The Spoon River Anthology, and The Complete History of America (abridged) in venues in Sheboygan, Wisconsin.

2010—Joe Ker, The Clown of Caricature. He is a caricature artist, who drew the Miller High Life man from the television ads.

2010—Mark and Dionne Alby Landgraf, with their daughter, Brooklyn Landgraf, and Dionne's sister, Kathy Alby.

Mark and Dionne Alby Landgraf with Brooklyn Landgraf and Kathy Alby

2010—Jeff and Kathy Anderson. Kathy works at the Sheboygan County Humane Society. She brings cats to the Memorial Mall on a weekend day, hoping that she'll find someone to adopt the animal.

Jeff and Kathy Anderson

2010—Fountain Park seemed crowded. Everyone is here for Earthfest, or the Farmer's Market, or both. Everyone looks like they are having fun. Plenty of food, music, plenty of other things to do.

the people

2010—Diane Bell, with her daughter.

Diane Bell with her daughter

2010—Paradigm Coffee & Music decided to use peddle power, instead of electricity, when mixing together blender drinks, like smoothies. The man with the yellow shirt is blending the drink.

2010—Matt Elliott was running for Sheboygan County Sheriff; he drove by, but didn't stop. He was a prison guard and supervisor for 17 years, he worked 8 years as an Elkhart Lake police officer, and ran the Security Arts Corporation for 18 years.

2010—Carol Rokicki is talking with friends. She works for the SASD.

Carol Rokicki

2010—Because of the large crowd, paramedics were available for emergencies.

the paramedics

2010—The Spotlight Theater performed "Cinderella Goes Disco."

2010—Robin Cardell and Kathy Alby. Robin had drumming/drum circles throughout the day.

2010—The second day of Earthfest, August 21. The tent-city is asleep right now, but at 10:30AM Barbara Hill will conduct an interdenominational spiritual service with "Lessons from the earth."

August 21, 2010

2010—Kathy Alby is ready for another day. The performers perform for free. After the Earthfest expenses are paid, the profit is donated to local charities.

Kathy Alby

AFTERWARD

Twenty-five years have gone by since I wrote the first press release for Kathy Alby's Earthfest. Everyone calls it Kathy Alby's Earthfest, but there are many volunteers and the coordinators that have helped it become successful.

I volunteered taking photos for Kathy. To make this book, I went through hundreds of photos, and I tried not to repeat myself, and if I did, it was to show how someone returned year after year to Earthfest, or how the parent returned with a child to the event. Earthfest evolved over the years. When the attendance was small, the people who attended were able to get to know one another, but as it grew, Toni Mattern told me she and her family stayed eight hours, there was so much to do.

Kathy reminds me of the woman who brought her own shopping bags shopping: she didn't care what others thought; she wanted to get the message out there. That reminds of me of Gaylord Nelson, the Senator from Wisconsin, who had a very difficult time, as well, to try to make people aware of the environment. When he started Earth Day on April 22, 1970, the public finally realized that what we do to the environment can affect us. Now, in Boston or Atlanta, or in other communities throughout the United States, these communities are celebrating Earth Day, or they have their own Earthfest. Again, each generation has to become aware of what they are doing the environment.

Earthfest is a great place to meet family and/or friends in a non-alcoholic environment, where the "natural highs" are drumming, yoga, or challenging the mind in how to think greener for today and the future.

Thanks to Jeff Ellair, Dyan Barbeau, or Karen McArdle at the UW-Sheboygan library. They were there to answer questions. Also, thanks to Jay or Jaime at Walgreens. They were great to help with any scanning problems and questions.

Finally, thanks to the Sheboygan County Historical Research Center in Sheboygan Falls, Wisconsin, for helping to bring this photographic history—the history of Earthfest—to life. It's important that other people see how Earthfest started out in 1990. And it's fun to see how it has progressed in the 20 years documented in the book.

Paul A. Hanson

PHOTO INDEX BY PAGES